I0802813

DISCOVERING JELLYFISH AND SEA SLUGS

by Charis Mather

BEARPORT PUBLISHING

Fusion Books, an imprint of Bearport Publishing by FlutterBee

Credits
All images are courtesy of Shutterstock.com, unless otherwise stated. Recurring – Net Vector, Baskiabat, NotionPic, PCH.Vector, Susann Guenther, LAtelier. Cover – Sahara Frost, KaenS, Mark-Anthony Falzon. 2–3 – boulham. 4–5 – MVshop, Mix Tape. 6–7 – Damsea, ali_kw, Kitjapat Film. 8–9 – RLS Photo, Anders Carlstrom. 10–11 – Andriy Nekrasov, DiveIvanov. 12–13 – Colorcocktail, Damsea, Jesus Cobaleda, Mark-Anthony Falzon. 14–15 – KaenS, SergeUWPhoto. 16–17 – Jesus Cobaleda, Mr. James Kelley. 18–19 – Martin Prochazkacz, Sahara Frost. 20–21 – Henryp982, Katherine Wallis. 22–23 – BlueOrange Studio, Simon Dannhauer.

Bearport Publishing Company Product Development Team
Kayla Eggert, Theresa Emminizer, Kim Jones, Allison Juda, Cole Nelson, Naomi Reich, Steve Scheluchin, Tiana Tran

Library of Congress Cataloging-in-Publication Data is available at www.loc.gov or upon request from the publisher.

ISBN: 979-8-89577-811-1 (hardcover)
ISBN: 979-8-89577-823-4 (ebook)

© 2026 BookLife Publishing
This edition is published by arrangement with BookLife Publishing.

North American adaptations © 2026 Bearport Publishing Company. All rights reserved. No part of this publication may be reproduced in whole or in part, stored in any retrieval system, or transmitted in any form or by any means, electronic, mechanical, photocopying, recording, or otherwise, without written permission from the publisher. Bearport Publishing is a division of FlutterBee Education Group.

For more information, write to Bearport Publishing, 3500 American Blvd W, Suite 150, Bloomington, MN 55431.
Printed in the United States of America.

CONTENTS

ALL ABOARD!

Ahoy there! Welcome to the See-Gulls Ocean Tours. We are about to set sail. Today, we are searching for squishy jellyfish and slimy sea slugs.

I am Captain Gulliver, and this is my trusty **crew**. We know about everything there is to see at sea. So, step aboard and let's begin our journey!

FOR YOUR INFORMATION

Like their land cousins, sea slugs are small, squishy, and slimy. They each have a strong foot, which they use to crawl around. But unlike land slugs, sea slugs live in salty water.

Jellyfish are also soft-bodied sea animals. They usually have bell-shaped bodies with lots of **tentacles**.

Sea slugs and jellyfish come in many bright colors and interesting shapes.

LION'S MANE JELLYFISH

Look at that jellyfish! It has many long, hairlike tentacles. That is why it's called a lion's mane jellyfish.

This jellyfish can have as many as 1,200 tentacles.

The lion's mane is one of the biggest jellyfish in the world. The largest one ever seen was 120 feet (37 m) long. Its tentacles have a powerful **venomous** sting.

SPANISH DANCERS

Next up is our first sea slug of the day, the Spanish dancer. Spanish dancers are bright red and frilly. When they move, their bodies flow like a dancer's dress.

Most sea slugs move by crawling, but some, like Spanish dancers, can swim.

Spanish dancers usually come out at night. During the day, they hide among the rocks where they lay their eggs.

Spanish dancers lay eggs in a ribbon-shaped clump.

FRIED EGG JELLYFISH

Have you ever seen a fried egg swim? Now you have. Well, it's not really a fried egg. It is a fried egg jellyfish! Fish sometimes hide under this jellyfish's oddly shaped bell.

Sometimes in warm weather, hundreds of fried egg jellyfish come together. This is called a bloom or a swarm.

The short, colorful tentacles of this jellyfish have only a mild sting.

LEAF SHEEP

Can you spy a tiny creature munching on green **algae**? This little cutie is called a leaf sheep slug!

This kind of sea slug is only about the size of a fingernail!

Leaf sheep slugs can do something special. After eating algae, they can turn sunlight into **energy.** This is the same way plants make their food!

UPSIDE-DOWN JELLYFISH

Is that jellyfish upside-down? It sure is! The upside-down jellyfish rests with its tentacles reaching up toward the sun.

Upside-down jellyfish get their energy from sunlight.

Watch out! This jellyfish can sting without even touching you. Upside-down jellyfish push out gobs of **mucus** that can sting small **prey** nearby.

BLUE DRAGONS

What a pretty blue dragon! These tiny sea slugs have feathery frills. To stay safe, they float in the water with their bellies facing up. This helps them blend in with the water around them.

Blue dragons have air in their bellies, which helps them float.

Blue dragons also stay safe another way. They store stinging cells in their bodies after eating sea creatures called Portuguese man-of-wars. This makes the blue dragons venomous, too!

A PORTUGUESE MAN-OF-WAR

BOX JELLYFISH

Box jellyfish may look harmless, but they are some of the most dangerous animals in the ocean. They are extremely venomous and can kill within minutes!

These jellyfish are named for the boxy shape of their bodies.

These deadly creatures are also fast swimmers. While most jellyfish just float around, box jellyfish can actually swim. They do this by pushing water in and out of their bodies.

BACK ON LAND!

Well, that was exciting! These jellyfish and sea slugs are all super interesting, but it's time to get back on dry land.

We hope that you will join us on another See-Gulls Ocean Tour soon. There is so much more to explore in the big blue sea! What animals will we find next time?

GLOSSARY

algae plantlike living things that are found in water

crew the group of people who work on a ship

energy the power that makes living things able to do things

mucus a sticky, slimy goo made by some animals

prey animals that are hunted by other animals for food

tentacles the long, bendy, armlike body parts of some animals

venomous able to poison another animal through a bite, sting, or scratch

INDEX